50 ...

BOOK SERIES
REVIEWS FROM READERS

I recently downloaded a couple of books from this series to read over the weekend thinking I would read just one or two. However, I so loved the books that I read all the six books I had downloaded in one go and ended up downloading a few more today. Written by different authors, the books offer practical advice on how you can perform or achieve certain goals in life, which in this case is how to have a better life.

The information is simple to digest and learn from, and is incredibly useful. There are also resources listed at the end of the book that you can use to get more information.

50 Things To Know To Have A Better Life: Self-Improvement Made Easy! by Dannii Cohen

---

This book is very helpful and provides simple tips on how to improve your everyday life. I found it to be useful in improving my overall attitude.

50 Things to Know For Your Mindfulness & Meditation Journey by Nina Edmondso

---

Quick read with 50 short and easy tips for what to think about before starting to homeschool.

50 Things to Know About Getting Started with Homeschool by Amanda Walton

I really enjoyed the voice of the narrator, she speaks in a soothing tone. The book is a really great reminder of things we might have known we could do during stressful times, but forgot over the years.

- HarmonyHawaii

50 Things to Know to Manage Your Stress: Relieve The Pressure and Return The Joy To Your Life

by Diane Whitbeck

There is so much waste in our society today. Everyone should be forced to read this book. I know I am passing it on to my family.

50 Things to Know to Downsize Your Life: How To Downsize, Organize, And Get Back to Basics

by Lisa Rusczyk Ed. D.

Great book to get you motivated and understand why you may be losing motivation. Great for that person who wants to start getting healthy, or just for you when you need motivation while having an established workout routine.

50 Things To Know To Stick With A Workout: Motivational Tips To Start The New You Today

by Sarah Hughes

50 THINGS TO KNOW ABOUT RIDING A BIKE

POINTS TO BE REMEMBERED ABOUT RIDING A BIKE

ANAND DHAKAL

Rochester (MN) Public Library

50 Things to Know About Riding a Bike Copyright © 2018 by CZYK Publishing LLC. All Rights Reserved.

All rights reserved. No part of this book may be reproduced in any form or by any electronic or mechanical means including information storage and retrieval systems, without permission in writing from the author. The only exception is by a reviewer, who may quote short excerpts in a review.

The statements in this book are of the authors and may not be the views of CZYK Publishing or 50 Things to Know.

Cover designed by: Ivana Stamenkovic
Cover Image: https://pixabay.com/en/mountains-motorcycle-ride-road-844871/

Edited by:

CZYK PUBLISHING

CZYK Publishing Since 2011.

50 Things to Know
Visit our website at www.50thingstoknow..com

Lock Haven, PA
All rights reserved.
ISBN: 9781728700663

50 THINGS TO KNOW ABOUT RIDING A BIKE

BOOK DESCRIPTION

Are you willing to learn about riding a bike safely, smoothly, and effectively?

Do you want complete knowledge about riding a bike?

Are you a bike lover? And wants to know in depth about a bike?

If you answered yes to any of these questions then this book is for you...

50 things to know about riding a bike by Anand Dhakal offers an approach to make you learn about riding a bike safely, smoothly, and effectively. Most books on this topic will only tell you limited points about a bike. You cannot find or you cannot learn in depth about a bike or about riding a bike. Although there's nothing wrong with that, they are also working to provide informative contents to all the readers. Based on knowledge from the world's leading experts and from my personal experience, I have mentioned 50 essential points that every bike riders should know.

In these pages, you'll discover all the essential 50 points about riding a bike. This book will help you to expand your knowledge about riding a bike safely, smoothly, and effectively.

By the time you finish this book, you will know a lot about riding a bike. It is very easy to ride a bike, but there are several things which all bike riders should be aware. So grab YOUR copy today. You'll be glad you did.

TABLE OF CONTENTS

50 Things to Know
Book Series
Reviews from Readers
BOOK DESCRIPTION
TABLE OF CONTENTS
ABOUT THE AUTHOR
INTRODUCTION
1. Learn completely about clutch and gear
2. Always wear shoes while riding a bike
3. Wearing Helmet is compulsory
4. Always use bike gloves
5. Practice on the ground, not on Highway
6. Never listen to songs while riding
7. Avoid answering phones
8. Do not ride the bike if you don't have a driving license
9. Ride slow
10. Pay tax consistently
11. Do insurance of your bike
12. Pay proper attention while riding a bike
13 Wait for a signal while overtaking a heavy vehicle
14. Always wear comfortable clothes
15. Always be sure that your petrol tank is full
16. Always put your key in the proper place

17. Do not show bike stunts on the highway
18. Always wear sunglasses
19. Do bike servicing every month
20. Do not blow unwanted horn
21. Make your tire tubeless
22. Cover your bike while parking in the open area
23. Always keep blood group certificate while riding a bike
24. Don't ride a bike if you are drunk
25. Always use a high-quality bike lubricant
26. Always check your tire before heading towards any places
27. Adjust your mirror
28. Also, pay attention to your mirror
29. Never overload your bike
30. Follow traffic rules
31. Avoid riding a bike in a rainy season
32. Always be aware of the local rules
33. Maintain distance
34. Educate yourself about all the traffic logos, sign, and symbols
35. Always carry money while riding a bike
36. Ride a bike which is comfortable
37. Take care of speed limit
38. Do not gossip with your passenger/friend
39. Be confident

50 Things to Know

40. Always carry the first-aid box
41. Always slow down your bike if you see small children
42. Do not panic after an accident
43. Never compete with other riders
44. Never try to hide your bike number plate
45. Use indicator while crossing the road
46. Ride safely in a foggy season
47. Turn off indicator
48. Use hand signal in a daytime
49. Check brakes before moving to any places
50. Lock your handle while parking in public places

Other Helpful Resources

50 Things to Know

ABOUT THE AUTHOR

Hello readers, I introduce myself as Anand Dhakal from a very beautiful country called Nepal. I was born in a city of Nepal called Biratnagar. I am a senior accountant in a non-life insurance company plus freelancer. I am a professional writer, accountant, transcriptionist, and translator. I love to write informative content because it will help to educate other people in the world. I love to spread information all over the world. It's my passion and I am very happy that I converted my passion into a profession.

A bike is the most beautiful thing in the world but if you fail to pay proper attention while riding a bike then it may surely result in an injury or even death. So I wrote this book to help you guys know more clearly about riding a bike. Riding a bike is simple but rider should have to know more deeply about it for smooth, and safe travel. I am motivated to write this book because I also suffered a lot because of a bike accident. It made me do rest on the bed for almost 6 months. So because of this reason, I am sharing 50 points which every bike riders should know. Every rider of the world should have to know these 50 points, and they should also follow these safety techniques for smooth, safe, and effective travel.

You can stay connected with me on Facebook: https://www.facebook.com/anand.dhakal.10

INTRODUCTION

If you worried about falling off the bike, you'd never get on.
Lance Armstrong

Hello readers, after reading this book series you will know all the essential things related to riding a bike. A bike is common all over the world and it is also a very convenient means of transportation. As it is of two-wheelers, there is a huge risk compared to four-wheelers. If you want to learn and know about riding a bike then this book is made for you.

Riding a bike seems easy but there are several points which we all riders should learn. In this book, I have mentioned 50 points that every rider should know. After reading this book, you will get huge knowledge about bike and you will know how to ride a bike safely.

Thus, in this book, you will find very informative content which will make you aware of riding a bike. There are several points mentioned in this book and most of the points are neglected by the riders. Safety should be given more priority. I also suffered a lot because of a bike accident. I rested on the bed for almost 6 months. So in this book, I am going to teach you 50 points about riding a bike safely, smoothly, and effectively.

1. LEARN COMPLETELY ABOUT CLUTCH AND GEAR

Clutch and gear are the most important things in the bike. You should be very confident in using clutch and gear of the bike. You have to increase the gear if you want to speed up your bike and also you have to decrease the gear if you want to slow down your bike. To change the gear you have to press the clutch and you should let go off the accelerator. You should be very fast while doing this process.

Never ride a bike if you are not totally confident because it may lead you to a big accident. First, you must have to do proper practice in the training ground then only you have to ride it on a road. Lack of confident will surely make you nervous while riding a bike. Clutch and gear are the heart of the bike, and it plays a great role while riding a bike.

2. ALWAYS WEAR SHOES WHILE RIDING A BIKE

Always wear shoes while riding a bike because it will minimize the risk of your legs from being injured. Never wear slippers while riding a bike because it increases the risk of your legs. If you wear slippers while riding a bike and unfortunately you had an accident then the skin of your legs can be injured. Wearing shoes while riding a bike also helps you to change the gears smoothly, and conveniently. Never use shoes of low quality and never wear uncomfortable shoes. Always try to wear a good quality and comfortable shoes. As it is directly concern to your safety issue you must not think about cheap and uncomfortable shoes. If you, unfortunately, had an accident then cheap shoes may result in expensive treatment. We can find different shoes which are mainly developed for riding a bike. So I suggest you buy that kind of shoes rather than normal shoes. And also wear shocks because it will absorb sweat produced by your leg and it also works to keep your feet warm in a winter season.

3. WEARING HELMET IS COMPULSORY

A helmet is the very important safety tools which will protect your head from being injured. For example, if someone had an accident then helmet can provide him/her a new life by protecting his/her head. Always wear a quality helmet, never go for a cheap helmet. A helmet is the most important safety tool, every bike riders should be aware of it. Always wear a full helmet so that it can protect your full head, never go for a half helmet. You can find several helmets in the market, don't wear helmets just to show off. Choose the one which is totally comfortable for your head and have the ability to fully protect your head. Thousands of people are dying every year in South Asian countries because of not wearing helmets.

You can mainly find helmets for these 3 vehicles. They are highlighted below:

1. Bicycle
2. Scooter
3. Motorbike

Always wear helmets according to your vehicles. Somewhat it will prevent you from losing your life if you had an accident.

4. ALWAYS USE BIKE GLOVES

Gloves are another important thing which every bike riders should use while riding a bike. If your hand is sweaty then it is very difficult for you to maintain grip, but gloves will prevent you from this difficulty. It will play a vital role in protecting your hand skin in case of an accident. We can find most of the people riding their bike without wearing gloves, it is disgusting. Everyone should be very much concern about their safety and security. Wearing gloves may seem simple and unwanted but it plays a big role in the time of the accident.

Why we should wear gloves while riding a bike? And here are the top reasons:

1. To maintain a grip
2. To protect your hand skin from being injured
3. To reduce the risk of an accident.
4. To ride a bike smoothly, conveniently, and safely.

5. PRACTICE ON THE GROUND, NOT ON HIGHWAY

If you want to practice riding a bike then always practice on the ground, not on the highway. Practicing on the highway may increase the risk of an accident. It will be very effective if you practice on the ground. Practicing on the ground will make you learn faster and it will be safer. If you have no any playground or any public ground then you should go to a training center. Never practice a bike on the highway or on the road but if you do so then you might face big trouble, not only you but you can create a trouble for a third party as well. Legally also you are not allowed to practice a bike on the road or highway. So if you do so you may charge certain fees and fines by the traffic police. Most of the accidental cases are happening in the world because of this reason. So it is better to practice a bike on the ground or you can go to a practice center.

6. NEVER LISTEN TO SONGS WHILE RIDING

You should not listen to songs while riding a bike because it will divert your mind and you may not pay proper attention. Listening to songs while riding a bike is the most common causes of the accident. You cannot hear the horn of other vehicles, every rider should avoid listening to songs while riding a bike. Most of the countries in the world are not giving permission to the riders to listen to songs while riding a bike. Listening songs while riding a bike will decrease your concentration, you cannot properly focus. You cannot know what is happening around you. You can listen to songs when you are free but never do so while riding a bike because it will surely increase the risk of your accident as well as it will create big trouble to the third party. So every rider in the world must be serious while riding a bike. Headsets and headphones are not invented to use while riding a bike.

7. AVOID ANSWERING PHONES

Phone calls are the most common and emerging cause of an accident. Always try to avoid answering every phone calls because it will increase the risk of an accident. If it is important then you can answer it but only after stopping your bike. Never answer the phone calls while riding a bike because you may lose your attention. You can put your phone on a bike mode. Bike mode will prevent you from unwanted calls, your phone will only ring if the call is very important. Legally also you are not allowed to answer a phone call while riding a bike but if you do so you may be punished by the traffic police. Somewhat Bluetooth devices can decrease the risk of an accident. But I strongly suggest you stop your bike in a safe place while answering your phone calls.

8. DO NOT RIDE THE BIKE IF YOU DON'T HAVE A DRIVING LICENSE

Driving license is the most important thing, if you have a driving license for a bike then you are capable of riding a bike. Please do not ride a bike if you don't have a driving license because you may fall in trouble if you meet an accident. If the mistake is done by other vehicles and you don't have a driving license then you will suffer a lot. If you lack driving license and you had an accident and the third party dies then you may be called as a killer and probably you may go to prison, but if you have a driving license then it is called an accident and the case can be solved very easily. And in the most of the countries, driving license is checked continuously by the traffic police. If they catch you then you have to pay handsome fees and fines to the traffic police. So first apply for a driving license and if you pass then only you should ride a bike on the highway.

9. RIDE SLOW

Do not ride a bike very fast because it will surely increase the risk of an accident. According to the global accident report, riding fast is the most common causes of an accident. Ride a bike according to the speed limit of the road. You can reach your destination if you ride a bike according to the speed limit of the road, but if you ride it very fast then it is not sure. If you exceed the speed limit of the road and unfortunately you faced an accident then it will be your mistake and your insurance company will not be responsible to bear the risk. So riders must be very much serious about the speed and should always ride a bike according to the speed limit of the road.

10. PAY TAX CONSISTENTLY

Paying tax is the duty of every citizen of the country. It will help the country to collect adequate public revenue. So it's the duty of all bike riders that you must pay your taxes consistently. If not then you may fall in trouble if you are checked by the traffic police. Paying tax is also the key points that every rider should be aware of it. As you are riding your bike on the road of your country so you must have to pay a certain amount of taxes to the government so that government can work for the development of the roads and infrastructure.

11. DO INSURANCE OF YOUR BIKE

Insurance is the process of sharing the risk. Insurance is the best method which will minimize the risk of your bike. It is compulsory that every rider should do their bike insurance. You have to pay a certain amount of money either monthly, quarterly or yearly (according to your country rules) to the insurance company and they will bear all the risk related to the bike. For example: If you hit another person by your bike then the insurance company will cover the financial problems according to their terms and conditions. In some countries there are rules that first you have to do insurance of your bike then only you are able to pay bike taxes to the government. Your insurance card, tax book, and driving license are regularly checked in almost every country in the world. So make sure that you have all these documents while riding a bike.

12. PAY PROPER ATTENTION WHILE RIDING A BIKE

Paying attention while riding a bike is a very important thing. Always pay proper attention while riding a bike. Do not look here and there because it will increase the risk of an accident. Concentrate properly and do not divert your mind. Always look ahead and pay a great attention because riding a bike is not a joke. You have to be very serious while riding a bike. If you lack your attention then it may create huge problems. Avoid listening to songs, answering phone calls, texting, etc. For the safe, convenient, and effective riding you must always be focused towards your destination.

13. WAIT FOR A SIGNAL WHILE OVERTAKING A HEAVY VEHICLE

Always wait for a signal while overtaking other heavy vehicles. Do not overtake without looking any signals because if you do so you may suffer from a huge trouble. You should wait for a signal of other vehicles and if the way is clear then only you should go ahead. You should be very serious while overtaking other vehicles because it is a very risky task. We can find many riders in a hurry and they just overtake other vehicles without looking any signals and this is the most common reason of an accident. You should not be in a hurry, always ride a bike with a cool mind and always wait for a signal of other vehicles.

14. ALWAYS WEAR COMFORTABLE CLOTHES

Comfortable clothes play a vital role in riding a bike smoothly, safely, and conveniently. Riding a bike is not simple, you should be very conscious of everything related to it. If the riders wear comfortable clothes while riding a bike then it will surely decrease the risk of an accident because comfortable clothes allow riders to change gear smoothly, maintain balance, and a lot more. You should always wear comfortable cloth while riding a bike. Never wear tight and difficult clothes because you may feel difficult while riding a bike.

15. ALWAYS BE SURE THAT YOUR PETROL TANK IS FULL

Sometimes we just ride a bike without checking the level of petrol and we fall in great trouble in the middle of our travel due to lack of petrol. Always check your petrol tank before going to any places. Never ride a bike when the petrol is very low because it may disturb you in the middle of your trip. Always be sure that your petrol tank is full, if not then you should fill it before moving to any places. It may seem simple but sometimes lack of petrol can create a huge problem.

For example: If you are going to give your first interview and you moved out of your house without even checking your petrol and in the middle of your travel you find that there is no gas or petrol in your bike. So can you imagine what will be your situation if the gas station is not nearby? You may lose an opportunity.

16. ALWAYS PUT YOUR KEY IN THE PROPER PLACE

Most of the riders are not putting their keys in the proper place where they can easily get. And when moving out they just search key everywhere. This is the problem of maximum riders and I know you have also experienced this. You should be very serious about your bike key. You should not place your key randomly in any places. You should put it in the proper place where you can easily find. This point seems simple but if you lose your key then sometimes it can create a huge problem. So always take care of your bike key and always put it in the proper place.

You can buy a key holder from the nearest market so that it will be easy for you to find out your key.

17. DO NOT SHOW BIKE STUNTS ON THE HIGHWAY

Majority of teenage riders are attracted towards bike stunts. They have a great passion for doing bike stunt. They like to show their skills to their family and friends but I request all the riders please do not show bike stunts on the road or highway because it increases the risk of an accident. If you want to do then you can do it on the ground or at the place where the bike stunt is performed. If you do bike stunts on the highway then there is a huge risk, due to such activity you can harm others and yourself as well. Doing bike stunts on the road or highway is also one of the common causes of an accident. In most of the Middle East and South Asian countries, you are not allowed to show your stunt skills on the road. Riders must be very much responsible and should avoid doing these kinds of activities.

18. ALWAYS WEAR SUNGLASSES

Sunglasses are another safety tools which will decrease the risk of an accident. Wearing sunglasses while riding a bike will prevent your eyes from dust and dirt. It will help you to maintain proper attention while riding a bike. If you fail to wear sunglasses then it can create several problems for you, your eyes can suffer from dust and dirt. At night also you should wear night vision sunglasses because at night there is a huge chance of getting insects into your eyes. In some helmets, we can find glasses too but if your helmet does not have a glasses then you should buy additional glasses. Always go for qualitative and advanced glasses. So for smooth riding a bike, you must have to wear sunglasses both in the daytime and the night time.

19. DO BIKE SERVICING EVERY MONTH

As we go to the doctor to do checkup either monthly, quarterly, or yearly, the same thing we should do for our bike. We should give our bike for servicing every month. Servicing of a bike is one of the most important things, and every bike riders should be aware of it. It is like a health checkup of the bike. Every month's bike should be given for a checkup so that it will be healthier and can run for several years. Servicing of the bike helps to detect all the defects of the bike. It will check everything such as a tire, brake, clutch, accelerator, and so on. You have to spend certain money for the proper maintenance of your bike. Spending certain money on servicing will surely prevent you from the big accident. It is better to spend some money today rather than spending huge money on your treatment. Thus, the bike should be given for checkup every month so that it will help to extend the lifespan of the bike and will allow you to ride your bike safely smoothly, and conveniently.

20. DO NOT BLOW UNWANTED HORN

Horn is the important thing which is used by every bike riders. Horn helps us to know that other vehicles need a way to move ahead. It helps to indicate that the vehicle is coming and it needs a way. But we should not blow unwanted bike horn because it creates a sound pollution, creates irritation, and also disturb the normal life of the people. In today's era, most of the countries have rules regarding the vehicle's horn. In most of the countries blowing unwanted horn is strictly banned. Due to constantly increasing in population vehicles are also increasing day by day which creates a huge sound pollution so it's our duty, and responsibility to not blow the unwanted horn. We should blow our bike horns when it is needed, we should not blow it continuously.

21. MAKE YOUR TIRE TUBELESS

Tubeless is another advance and new way to protect your tire from being punctured. So every rider should make their bike tire tubeless because it will help them to prevent their tire from being punctured and from other tire damages. In a tubeless tire, it lacks a tube inside the tire and instead of the tube, there are liquid chemicals. So due to this reason, you will not face the problem like puncture but you should check your tire regularly before moving to any places. If there is any nails or glasses attached to your tire then you should make your tire free from that. Tubeless tires play a vital role in the smooth running of the bike.

For example: If you are going to the place which is 100 kilometers away and your tire is not tubeless. So while riding a bike if any nails or glasses attached to your tire then it will suddenly make your tire puncture. And if there is no any repair centers nearby, what you will do now? So it is better to make your tire tubeless.

22. COVER YOUR BIKE WHILE PARKING IN THE OPEN AREA

Every rider must be careful and should be serious about their bike. You should keep your bike clean and tidy so due to this reason always cover your bike while parking in the open area. In most of the cases you can get your bike covers at the time of purchasing a bike but if you don't have then you must have to buy compulsory from the nearest market. Bike covers also help in extending the lifespan of a bike because it keeps dust and dirt away from it. Bike cover also helps to keep the paint of the bike fresh and clean. You should always carry your bike covers whenever you are going outside. Thus, Bike cover is the essential thing and it must be used by every bike riders.

23. ALWAYS KEEP BLOOD GROUP CERTIFICATE WHILE RIDING A BIKE

Blood certificate is very much important document which you should carry while riding a bike. Riding a bike is not a joke, if you fail to give proper attention while riding a bike then you can suffer from a huge problem. So it is compulsory that every bike rider must keep their blood group certificate with them. If you keep your blood group certificate with you while riding a bike then it will help a lot in an emergency case. This is a simple point but it can help you a lot.

For example: If you faced an accident while riding a bike then by the help of your blood group certificate the police will know who you are, where are you from, and what is your blood group. You can get immediate treatment which can save your life.

24. DON'T RIDE A BIKE IF YOU ARE DRUNK

Riding a bike when you are drunk is the most dangerous things. Your hand, feet, and a whole body cannot be in a condition to ride a bike. You cannot control your bike properly and effectively but if you do so you may face an accident which will harm you and to the third party as well. This is also one of the most common causes of an accident. Please never ride a bike if you are drunk because it will help you to prevent a big accident. If you are drunk then it is better to avoid riding a bike because you cannot ride your bike safely when you are drunk. In most of the countries it is against the law, you may be punished if you ride a bike after consuming alcohol or you may have to pay certain fines and penalties to the government.

25. ALWAYS USE A HIGH-QUALITY BIKE LUBRICANT

Lubricant plays a great role in making your engine healthier. You can find several types of bike lubricants from cheaper to expensive. Never use low-quality bike lubricants because it will degrade the health of your bike. Always choose quality lubricants because it will make your engine smoother and healthier. Not every cheaper product are low quality and not very expensive products are high quality. Never judge the products according to the price. Choose the qualitative lubricants to protect your bike engine so that you can ride your bike safely, smoothly, and more effectively.

26. ALWAYS CHECK YOUR TIRE BEFORE HEADING TOWARDS ANY PLACES

Although your tire is tubeless you need to check it before riding a bike so that you cannot fall into any trouble in the middle of your trip. Every rider must be responsible and serious, so you should not go anywhere without checking your tire. You have to see whether there are nails, screws, or other harmful things that are attached to your tire or not. If there are such harmful things then you have to make your tire free from that. But if are unable to free your tire from these harmful things then you need to go to your nearby repair centers. If you do careless and move out without checking your tire then there are huge chances of blowing out which can seriously make you injured, this point may seem very simple but it can save your life and can prevent you from getting into a big trouble.

27. ADJUST YOUR MIRROR

Mirror of your bike is another safety tool which will protect you and save you from an accident. I have seen many riders riding their bike without caring about the importance of the mirror. Always adjust your mirror before going to any places because mirror will tell you what's going on your back. You can see the objects from your mirror and it will also help you in crossing the road. Always see your mirror of your bike before crossing the road. You should also clean your bike mirror and should make it clear. Most of the accidental cases occurring in South Asia is because of the unadjusted mirror. So before going to any places, you must have to adjust your mirror properly so that you can ride safely and smoothly.

28. ALSO, PAY ATTENTION TO YOUR MIRROR

First, you must have to adjust your mirror properly and after that, you need to pay attention to the mirror as well. Riding a bike may seem simple but you have to pay a great attention towards many things. So paying attention towards your mirror is also compulsory, it will save you from a big trouble. Never cross your road or never overtake any vehicles without looking your mirror. With the help of a mirror, you can see the objects coming towards you. Mirrors are given so that you can look back and can know what is going on your back so every rider must utilize their mirror properly and effectively. You should not be careless, you should pay attention to many things. But if you fail to do so then it will surely create a big trouble for you. You will surely face an accident and it may result in serious injury or even death. So it is very important to pay an attention towards your mirror while riding a bike.

29. NEVER OVERLOAD YOUR BIKE

Another main cause of an accident is overload. Many riders do not care about this, they just carry their family, and friends in their bike. Yes, we need to carry our family, and friends but not more than our bike capacity. You can carry your one friends along with you while riding a bike. Always ride a bike safely, never overload it. A bike is mainly made for only two people i.e. one is rider and other is a passenger. Overload may disturb you while riding a bike and it can result in a big accident. In some countries, you can see only one person riding a bike but in some countries, you can find two people, one is a rider and the other is a passenger. But do not carry more than one people on your bike because you are not legally allowed and it will increase the risk of an accident. You must be responsible and serious because riding a bike is not a joke. If you overload your bike then you have to surely pay a certain amount of money as fines and penalties to the traffic police, and you may lose your driving license too. Therefore, please never overload your bike.

30. FOLLOW TRAFFIC RULES

Every rider must know all the traffic rules, symbols, and regulation of the countries. You must be educated about this and must follow it compulsory because traffic rules are designed for our safety and security. This will prevent you from an accident. Never be in a hurry always follow the rules and regulation. What will you do by saving 5 seconds of your life? Never neglect traffic rules as it is concerned for our safety and security. Different countries have different traffic rules, we must obey it so that we can travel from one place to other safely and smoothly. Majority of the countries charge fine to the one who breaks the traffic rules, it is also our duty and responsibility to follow the traffic rules.

31. AVOID RIDING A BIKE IN A RAINY SEASON

It is not possible to completely avoid riding a bike in a rainy season but somewhat you can minimize or reduce it. A bike is a very convenient means of transportation but as it is made of two-wheelers it has a high risk as compared to four-wheelers. You should not ride a bike in a rainy season because it has the high risk of an accident. In a rainy season, the road will be very slippery which will increase the risk of an accident. If your tire does not have a proper grip then you can suffer from a big trouble. If you can't avoid riding a bike in a rainy season then you should use the tire which has better grip. Grip will help you to maintain balance while riding a bike. You should also be very serious and should be focused on your destination. Riders should ride a bike at an average speed. So it's better to minimize riding a bike in a rainy season but if it is possible to avoid then you must avoid it in a rainy season.

32. ALWAYS BE AWARE OF THE LOCAL RULES

Every rider must know the rules and regulation of their final destination. Riders should have enough knowledge about local rules and regulations. There are different rules for riding a bike within a country. You can find one rule in one state and another rule in another state. So you must be aware of it before moving to the new places. Some state of Nepal does not allow you to blow a horn and some state of Nepal does not allow you to cross the speed limit. Riders should do proper research about their destination and should follow that. If you have no any knowledge about the rules and regulation of your destination then you may fall in a big trouble. There are several different rules in different places so you must be aware of the local rules and the regulation. To know about the local rules and regulations you should check it on the internet or you can buy a book about the traffic rules and regulations.

33. MAINTAIN DISTANCE

Maintaining distance is one of the safety measures to avoid an accident. Riders must maintain distance from other vehicles but if you fail to maintain the distance then you may face an accident. Never go close to other vehicles because if suddenly other vehicle stops then you may suffer from a big trouble. Always try to ride a bike 3 seconds behind other vehicles. Avoid going close to other vehicles because it is also one of the burning causes of an accident. We can see many riders going close to other vehicles without any fear but 70% of these kinds of riders will surely face an accident. So it is always better to maintain distance while riding a bike.

34. EDUCATE YOURSELF ABOUT ALL THE TRAFFIC LOGOS, SIGN, AND SYMBOLS

Riders should have knowledge of all the traffic logos, sign, and symbols because they have to deal with it every day while riding a bike. A person is not considered as a rider if he lacks the knowledge of traffic logos, sign, and symbols. You can see various different traffic logos, sign, and symbols on the road, if you don't know the meaning of the logos then it will be very difficult for you. You may fall in a big trouble, you should know the meaning of all the traffic logos. You have to educate yourself before riding a bike. I request you all bike rider to not ride a bike if you don't know the meaning of traffic logos. So educate yourself about all the traffic logos because it can save your life.

For example, James is traveling to the New York City and in between, he saw a red light but he ignores it because he doesn't know the meaning of the red light and he moved continuously. So now can you imagine what is going to happen with James?

I am going to mention some of the meaning of traffic logos, sign, and symbols. But in detail, you need to research more.

1. Red light: Means you have to stop your bike
2. Green light: You can go
3. Yellow light: Yellow light indicates that red light is going to turn on. In this condition either you can stop or you can go. But you have to go before it turns red.

35. ALWAYS CARRY MONEY WHILE RIDING A BIKE

Money is useful everywhere and it is even more useful if you are riding a bike. You can face several difficulties and problems on the go. You should always carry a certain amount of money with you while riding a bike because it can be useful if your bike fails to perform. Money can be useful if you had an accident. Money can also be useful to fill your fuel tank if it is getting low. Please don't ride a bike without carrying a money because money can be used at any time while riding a bike. It is better to carry cash amount instead of cards because you can instantly use your money if you face any problems and difficulties and hence it will save your time too. As we humans don't know when we will fall ill then it is a machine it can create problems at any time so it is very important to carry a certain amount of money while riding a bike.

36. RIDE A BIKE WHICH IS COMFORTABLE

A bike is a convenient means of transportation and it is used by a huge number of population all over the world. An individual should have to select a bike which is comfortable for him/her. If the individual height is short then he/she have to select and ride a bike which is short, if the individuals are energetic and can control the pressure of the bike then he/she can ride heavy bikes. I have seen many riders most of them are teenagers riding a very heavy bike which is beyond their control. It will increase the risk of an accident so always ride a bike which is comfortable for you. If you can't ride a heavy bike then please don't go for it. Always choose a bike according to your comfort so that you can ride it smoothly, safely, and more conveniently. So always ride a bike which is comfortable for you, don't choose a bike according to the latest trend.

37. TAKE CARE OF SPEED LIMIT

If you are a rider then you have to be careful about many things. A speed of bike should not exceed the speed limit of the road. A speed limit is calculated by evaluating every aspect of the road. If you exceed the speed limit it means you are increasing the risk of an accident. You may also have to pay a certain amount of money as fines and penalties to the traffic police if you fail to follow the traffic rules. As different roads have a different speed limit and you should ride according to that. Never cross the speed limit because it is our duty and responsibility to obey the traffic rules and regulations.

For example, suppose you crossed the speed limit and you had an accident, so in this case, your insurance company will not bear your risk because you avoided the rules and regulation. So it is very important to ride a bike according to the speed limit of the roads.

38. DO NOT GOSSIP WITH YOUR PASSENGER/FRIEND

Riding a bike is not a joke, you must be serious and responsible. You should not gossip with your passenger/friend while riding a bike because you may lack concentration and it may result in a serious injury or even death. I have seen many people gossiping with their friends or passengers while riding a bike, it is very dangerous. Safety and security should be given first priority. Gossiping with friends while riding a bike is also one of the main cause of an accident. A rider must be focused on his/her destination. For safe, smooth, and effective traveling rider should not involve in gossiping with his/her friends. You can gossip with your passenger/friend when you stop your bike, so please avoid gossiping with your passenger/friend while riding a bike.

39. BE CONFIDENT

Always be confident while riding a bike. Don't be nervous by looking at the traffic. If you are not totally confident then please do not ride a bike on the highway. First, practice a lot on the ground or in a practice center before riding on the road. To be confident you must have to know each and everything of the bike. Lack of confident can increase the risk of your accident and it may harm you and the third party as well. So you should be confident while riding a bike.

40. ALWAYS CARRY THE FIRST-AID BOX

Riding a bike is a risky task. If you fail to concentrate and pay attention while riding a bike then you may fall in a trouble. If you are a very responsible rider but also sometimes due to other rider's mistake you may fall in trouble. So due to these reasons, you should always carry your first aid box while riding. Sometimes your first aid box can be useful for other riders too. The first-hand box can be useful at any time. Many bike riders ignore it but it is very important to carry the first-aid box. Suppose if someone had an accident and if he/she has a first-aid box then it can be used before going to the hospital. It is better to go hospital after taking first-aid treatment rather going directly. Sometimes the first-aid box can save the life of the rider.

41. ALWAYS SLOW DOWN YOUR BIKE IF YOU SEE SMALL CHILDREN

Small children are very cute. They are too small that they cannot evaluate what is wrong, and what is right. You should always ride a bike according to the speed limit of the road but when you see children on the road then you must have to slow your bike. Children mind is not totally developed, they can cross the road without looking at anything, they can run on a road, they can even play in a road. So you must be conscious about it. Children will not care what is coming they will just run so if you slow down your bike then it may save the life of the children. Not decreasing the speed of a bike when the children is around is one of the reason of an accident. Many children around the world had sacrificed their life. Children are the gift of the god, they are innocent and their mind is not totally developed but our mind is developed so we must have to think about it and should always slow our bike when we see small children.

42. DO NOT PANIC AFTER AN ACCIDENT

An accident can happen at any time at anywhere if you fail to concentrate while riding a bike. Sometimes you might face an accident because of other rider's mistake. But always keep in mind that you should not panic because it will generate more trouble for you. If you get into an accident always try to stay calm and never panic. Panic will definitely not solve your problem, you should be cool and calm. Panic may cause another health problem so always try to be cool after an accident. We may have seen or heard many cases where rider dies because of a heart attack. Sometimes panic may result in a heart attack too. If you panic then it will be so hard to control the situation. You should call police and ambulance immediately after an accident and always try to avoid discussing an accident with the local people.

43. NEVER COMPETE WITH OTHER RIDERS

If you are riding a bike then it does not mean that you have to compete with others. We have seen many riders doing competition especially teenagers are more attracted towards it. Stop competing with others. Riders must be serious and should be responsible while riding a bike. Doing competition with other riders is also one of the biggest causes of an accident. Always ride according to your skill and talent. Never try to compete with other riders because it will increase the huge risk of an accident. If you want competition then take part in road race sport but never compete with others on the road or highway. If you do so then it may create problems for you and for the third party as well. Your life is precious so never try to waste it by doing these kinds of activities. These kinds of competition won't make you superior. So everyone should be concern about it and should avoid this kind of activity.

44. NEVER TRY TO HIDE YOUR BIKE NUMBER PLATE

The number plate is an identity of your bike. The number plate is unique and you should never try to hide your bike number plate, make sure that your number plate is clearly visible. Never try to cheat by hiding the number plate. It's your duty to make your number plate visible. Your thinking must not be negative, a rider must be positive and they should be responsible and humble. Breaking the law by hiding a number plate is termed as a crime. So riders must not be a cheater, they should have a positive mind. As we can see several modern bikes where the number plate is very small. These kinds of bikes are banned in Nepal and in many countries. In Nepal, you have to show your bike number plate clearly. If you fail to do so then you have to pay fines and penalties to the traffic police.

45. USE INDICATOR WHILE CROSSING THE ROAD

Indicators are also one of the safety tools which help you to prevent an accident. The indicator helps other riders behind you, they can know in which direction you are going with the help of this small indicators lights. Always use indicator while crossing the road. Never cross the road without blinking your indicator. For example, if you want to go left then blink your left indicator because indicator tells other riders that your bike is moving in the left direction so that other riders will be aware of that. But don't cross the road directly without blinking your indicator because sometime some other vehicle may be at a great speed so if you do so it may result in an accident. So you must see your mirror first and if everything is okay then blink your indicator and cross the road. After crossing the road you must have to turn off your indicators light.

46. RIDE SAFELY IN A FOGGY SEASON

A foggy season is one of the most dangerous seasons for every bike riders. We can hear most of the accident cases in a foggy season. Riding a bike in a foggy season is very difficult. You cannot see what is ahead of your bike until and unless that vehicle is closer to you. You should ride very sincerely, you should not be in a hurry while riding a bike in a foggy season. Always glow your headlight while riding in a foggy season because this will helps other vehicles to know that you are coming. You should ride a bike slowly in a foggy season. You must try to minimize riding a bike in a foggy season because there is a huge risk of an accident but if it is not possible to minimize and it is very important then you must pay a proper attention, and you must be focused while riding a bike in a foggy season.

47. TURN OFF INDICATOR

We may have seen many riders who just keep on glowing their indicators light which create a big problem for other vehicles. After using indicator you must turn it off. Riders should be serious and should pay attention to everything while riding a bike. They must have to turn off their indicators light without forgetting. If you forget to turn off your indicators light then it will create a huge confusion for other riders. They will be confused and they will fail to determine that where you want to cross. So you must turn it off immediately after crossing the road. Due to this reason sometime it may result in an accident, for example, if you want to move in a left direction and you blinked your left indicator, and after crossing the road you forgot to turn off your indicator. So, in this case, other vehicles behind you will think that you are again moving in a left direction and they may overtake you from the right direction. So if this happens then it may result in a serious injury and sometime it may also result in a death.

48. USE HAND SIGNAL IN A DAYTIME

Indicators help you in crossing the road but it is not more effective in a daytime. Sometime you must have to use your hand too. Always don't depend upon indicator while crossing the road because in a daytime due to sunlight other riders may not see your indicator light. So, in this case, you must have to use your hand for a signal. If you will not use your hand while crossing the road in a daytime then you may face an accident. This point is simple but it will prevent you from a big accident.

How to use a hand signal? So the answer to this question is mentioned below:

For example: If you want to go in a right direction then blink your right indicator and after blinking your indicator you must use your right hand for the signal. This point may seem simple but it is one of the best safety technique.

49. CHECK BRAKES BEFORE MOVING TO ANY PLACES

Brakes are the backbone of the bike. Brakes help you to stop your bike wherever you want. But sometimes we may hear the term 'Break fail'. If your break fail to perform then you will surely fall into a big trouble. So do not ride a bike without checking your brakes. Always be sure that your brakes are working properly before moving to any places. Brakes are the most important part of the bike, and every rider must check their both hand and foot brake before heading towards any places because it can save the life of the rider, and of the third party as well. Most of the people ride a bike without checking brakes, tire, petrol, and other bike equipment, they must have to erase this kind of habits. We regularly hear different accidental cases because of failure of the brake. A brake is a machine and sometime it may not work so it is compulsory to check it before moving to any places.

50. LOCK YOUR HANDLE WHILE PARKING IN PUBLIC PLACES

Nowadays if you have a good looking bike then there are huge chances of being stolen. You should take good care of your bike. You must be responsible and serious, you should provide a good security for your bike. A person is said to be a good rider if he/she pay proper attention to the security of his/her bike. So never park your bike in a public place without locking your handle. You must lock your handle because it increases the safety of your bike. You can use an additional lock for your bike by purchasing it from the nearest market. Always pay proper attention while parking your bike in a public place, a thieve can easily break your basic lock system so always try to use advance lock system. In today's world, we can find different advance lock system for our bike which we can purchase from our nearest market. So it is very much important to lock your bike handle by advance lock system while parking in a public place.

OTHER HELPFUL RESOURCES

1. 10 Tips For Riding Any Bike, The First Time: https://rideapart.com/articles/10-tips-riding-any-bike-the-first-time-without-looking-like-idiot

2. Top 10 Motorcycle safety tips: https://www.seeker.com/top-10-motorcycle-safety-tips-1765348725.html

3. 25 tips for safe riding in heavy traffic: https://www.bikedekho.com/advisory/25-tips-for-safe-riding-in-heavy-traffic.htm

50 Things to Know

READ OTHER

50 THINGS TO KNOW

BOOKS

50 Things to Know to Get Things Done Fast: Easy Tips for Success

50 Things to Know About Going Green: Simple Changes to Start Today

50 Things to Know to Live a Happy Life Series

50 Things to Know to Organize Your Life: A Quick Start Guide to Declutter, Organize, and Live Simply

50 Things to Know About Being a Minimalist: Downsize, Organize, and Live Your Life

50 Things to Know About Speed Cleaning: How to Tidy Your Home in Minutes

50 Things to Know About Choosing the Right Path in Life

50 Things to Know to Get Rid of Clutter in Your Life: Evaluate, Purge, and Enjoy Living

50 Things to Know About Journal Writing: Exploring Your Innermost Thoughts & Feelings

50 Things to Know

Website: 50thingstoknow.com

Facebook: facebook.com/50thingstoknow

Pinterest: pinterest.com/lbrennec

YouTube: youtube.com/user/50ThingsToKnow

Twitter: twitter.com/50ttk

Mailing List: Join the 50 Things to Know Mailing List to Learn About New Releases

50 Things to Know

Please leave your honest review of this book on Amazon and Goodreads. We appreciate your positive and constructive feedback. Thank you.

CPSIA information can be obtained
at www.ICGtesting.com
Printed in the USA
LVHW091434081118
596432LV00001B/187/P

9 781728 700663